Trading Forex

Introduction and Basic Strategies

By

John Gibson

Copyright 2018 by John Gibson - All rights reserved.

The following book is reproduced below with the goal of providing information that is as accurate and reliable as possible. Regardless, purchasing this book can be seen as consent to the fact that both the publisher and the author of this book are in no way experts on the topics discussed within and that any recommendations or suggestions that are made herein are for entertainment purposes only. Professionals should be consulted as needed prior to undertaking any of the action endorsed herein.

This declaration is deemed fair and valid by both the American Bar Association and the Committee of Publishers Association and is legally binding throughout the United States.

Furthermore, the transmission, duplication or reproduction of any of the following work including specific information will be considered an illegal act irrespective of if it is done electronically or in print. This extends to creating a secondary or tertiary copy of the work or a recorded copy and is only allowed with express written consent from the Publisher. All additional right reserved.

The information in the following pages is broadly considered to be a truthful and accurate account of facts and as such any inattention, use or misuse of the information in question by the reader will render any resulting actions solely under their purview. There are no scenarios in which the publisher or the original author of this work can be in any fashion deemed liable for any hardship or damages that may befall them after undertaking information described herein.

Additionally, the information in the following pages is intended only for informational purposes and should thus be thought of as universal. As befitting its nature, it is presented without assurance regarding its prolonged validity or interim quality. Trademarks that are mentioned are done without written consent and can in no way be considered an endorsement from the trademark holder.

Table of Contents

Introduction 4

Chapter 1: The Forex Market 7

Chapter 2: Market Mechanics 13

Chapter 3: The Basics- Trends and Ranges 24

Chapter 4: Turning Points 33

Chapter 5: The MACD- Improved 39

Chapter 6: 20 EMA S/R 47

Chapter 7: Momentum Patterns 52

Chapter 8: Price Action Patterns 67

Chapter 9: Risk Management 86

Chapter 10: Mindset and Success 100

Chapter 11: How to Make Millions 110

Introduction

Hello and thank you for buying this book. Chances are you have some knowledge of the financial markets and have some experience trading them whether as a beginner, an expert or as is most common, the frustrated semi professional. The odds are also good that the biggest reason you decided to start trading in the first place is because of the massive financial rewards it offers. You may be passionate about the markets and the way they work but, to be honest, passion doesn't quite match the feeling of knowing you can make a living in the markets and that you can rely upon yourself to create a richer life using your skills in trading.

Well, I'm here to hammer a few home truths into you. Yes, trading offers massive financial rewards. Rewards which only a few can ever hope to achieve. Getting there though is a function of passion, hard work and time. If you're expecting millions per month after reading a book like this, well, you're probably better off "investing" in the hot business idea du jour. Let me make this clear: To obtain the rewards you need to master a variety of skills. Technical skills, Risk management skills and most importantly mindset.

The good news is this: Trading successfully is a process. It involves executing a number of steps perfectly and managing your expectations regarding outcomes you have no control over. It involves understanding the risks you undertake every time you sit to trade and mitigating them as best as you can. It involves training yourself to be aware of what is inside your head and how that affects you. This book, the first of a series, is an attempt to demystify these skills of successful trading across the currency and derivative markets. In this book, we will focus on the basics of how the FX market works and some basic strategies you can utilize.

We will first look at the mechanics and character of the FX market before diving into some basics skills you need to have before we begin looking at strategies. After that, we will look at risk management techniques and round it all off with a brief look at mindset management. The full topic of mindset is beyond the scope of this single book and will be addressed in later books in this series.

Do whatever you need to do to understand the material in here. Study it, print it out, buy a print version and re-read it multiple times. This is a very dense book and some topics will take time to understand, especially the basics. With that being said: I wish you the best of luck in your journey to trade successfully. Always remember: You're a lot closer than you believe. Always.

Chapter 1: The Forex Market

Off all the financial markets operating in the world, the forex market has the highest turnover on a daily basis. At $4 trillion per day, it dwarfs even the institutional bond and fixed income market which is where the big boys come out to play. The Forex market is a mixture of institutions (like hedge funds, bank trading desks etc), central banks (in this age of quantitative easing) and retail traders. While there aren't any exact figures available, the overall size of the market ensures liquidity at most times.

This is significant to note because unlike the stock markets, the forex market is a 24 hour market. The official open is Monday 8AM Tokyo time and the official close is Friday 5PM New York time. So the market essentially stays open all week except for Saturdays with multiple sessions opening and closing everyday. There is some light trading which happens late on a Sunday but from a beginner's standpoint this can be ignored since volumes are low and liquidity is sketchy. The instruments one can trade are currency pairs involving pretty much every currency around the world. The only limit to what you can trade is determined by which pairs your broker chooses to make available. The pairs can be divided into 3 major categories.

The first category is called the "Majors" and refer to the pairing of the US Dollar with the following currencies: The Australian dollar, New Zealand Dollar, Japanese Yen, Swiss Franc, Canadian Dollar, British Pound and the Euro. The Euro/British pound pair and the Euro/Japanese Yen pair are considered majors in addition to the above. Then come the "minors" which are crosses between these currencies themselves like the Euro/Aussie Dollar, Pound/New Zealand dollar, Swiss Franc/Japanese Yen etc. The minors are larger in number compared to the majors. Lastly, we have the "exotics" which involve currencies like the Thai Baht or the Russian Ruble or South African Rand which are thinly traded and are extremely volatile i.e. they tend to jump around a lot and have less liquidity.

Trading volume wise, the Euro/USD is the most heavily traded followed by the major pairs. The minor pairs have good volumes as well and see greater volumes during the times that country's markets are open. For example: the pound/Swiss franc will see huge volumes when European markets are open with volumes tailing away towards the end of the New York close. On a 24 hour basis, the market can be divided into 3 major sessions which last about 9 hours each with some overlap. The 24 hour cycle is considered to start with the Tokyo open and is referred to as the Asian session. The Asian session includes the markets in Japan, China, Singapore, Hong Kong, New Zealand and Australia. Technically Auckland (in New Zealand) opens prior to Tokyo but that's being a bit pedantic. Major volumes kick in when Sydney, Tokyo and Hong Kong open. The Asian session is considered closed with the closing of the Tokyo and Hong Kong markets. The final hour of the Asian session overlaps with the first hour of the next session, the European session. The European session officially opens in Geneva, Switzerland but volumes really kick in when London opens. The European session sees the highest trading volumes of the day since it overlaps with both the previous Asian session and the next, New York session.

The European and New York sessions share an overlap of almost 4 hours, that is, the post lunch session of London and the morning session in New York, and these 4 hours witness the highest liquidity and volumes of the day across all currencies except some of the Asian pairs and the exotics. London closes at lunch time New York (roughly 12 PM) and the session continues to see decent volumes despite a drop off. New York closes at 5PM EST and though the market is officially considered closed for the day, trading does take place as San Francisco and Dallas remain open past New York close. There is a gap of an hour or so where no major market is open before Auckland and Tokyo open and the next day begins.

Please note: though I use the word open and close, this only refers to the local markets. The overall market is still considered open and it is possible to place trades until Friday 5PM New York. Technically, the weekly close is a little later than that but practically speaking, volumes see a major plunge and it isn't worth trading past that time. This range of opens and closes creates an interesting dynamic of volatility and liquidity with certain strategies playing better at certain times and under performing at others. An FX trader should always be aware of what session they're currently in and how volumes will be impacted for the pairs they trade.

Speaking of volumes, unlike equity markets, the FX market does not have a single centralized order book. This is because there is no central exchange, like the NYSE or NASDAQ, where orders are matched together and executed. The Forex market is an interconnected network of dealers. This means a dealer (that is provider of currency or liquidity provider) doesn't have access to the next dealer's volumes and may not even be connected to all dealers in the network. There are some providers which offer volume data to institutions but even they offer volumes only on a few pairs and even that isn't the entire data. This is a major deviation from the stock markets and often flummoxes even successful equity traders since volumes cannot be relied upon and a whole host of derivative indicators like the Acc/Dis etc are not as accurate.

The FX markets also present another challenge to the equity trader since there is no hard close and positions can continue to be actively traded well past the trader's bed time. This causes some traders to think they need to be glued to the terminal for 18 hour stretches but as we'll see later, this need not be the case unless one consciously chooses to do so. Holidays provide interesting dynamics as well since it is entirely possible that while one market is on holiday and is closed, the next one is open. Thus, the price action and order characteristics may be unreliable and any strategy that needs to be backtested has to take this into account.

The mechanics of the FX market, in short, are very different to the stock markets. The next chapter details these differences beginning with a very basic one. The spread and what it means.

Chapter 2: Market Mechanics

While on the surface the forex market may appear to be similar to the stock market, underneath it all, there are very different mechanisms at play. Part of this has to do with the non centralized nature of the market and part of it has to do with the types of players in the market. The stock market never witnesses any sort of intervention from institutions like central banks. Any insider trading that occurs in the stock market is also declared and can be followed pretty easily. Forex brokers too are a different breed from their stock market counterparts. While stock brokers are pretty heavily regulated across all markets, this is not really the case with forex brokers. Sure, brokers in reputable jurisdictions like the US, UK and Australia etc are subject to the same regulatory scrutiny but the vast majority of FX brokers are domiciled in the offshore tax havens of the world.

This is not to say all such brokers are disreputable. It just means you need to do your research in more depth since broker choice is a lot more crucial in FX than in stocks. You'll often find the large majority of FX brokers advertise the fact that they don't charge commission. Zero commission brokers simply do not exist in the stock markets. Neither do they exist in the FX market despite what they may claim. The reality is that the commission is built into the price spread. Those of you unfamiliar with what a spread is: Buying and selling is never done at the same price. As a trader, you will buy at what is known as the "ask" or "offer" price and sell at what's called the "bid" price. These bid/ask prices are given to you by the broker and the difference between the bid/ask is called the spread. Greater the spread, the more distance your trades need to travel to earn a profit.

A majority of FX brokers simply build the commission into the spread by tacking on a few extra points into the spread and then advertise it as zero commission. They can do this because without a central order book, there isn't any central price matching engine running which can see all prices in the market and thus prevent anyone from quoting prices which are off by too much from the current market fair price. All brokers which offer this type of deal are engaging in a practice known as "B" booking. In stock markets, brokers are not allowed to trade against their clients if the client's account is below a certain size. This is true of all the markets of developed countries. The FX market though escapes such scrutiny which enables the broker to trade against you and thus, profits off you on much more than just the commission.

There are hybrid brokers as well who practice both "A" and "B" booking. "A" booking refers to orders which are passed on directly to the broker's liquidity provider (usually a large financial institution) and you'll find such hybrid brokers "A" book the trades of clients who are profitable and above a certain account value, usually, above 10k USD. The broker's reasoning is that since the vast majority of FX accounts are small and since most clients go bust within a year, they might as well make hay while the client has some funds in their account. While legal, this practice is quite sketchy and puts the odds of success against the smaller trader or unprofitable trader. I highly recommend opening accounts only with "STP" brokers. STP stands for straight through processing i.e where orders are sent directly to the liquidity providers and all the broker makes is a commission. It is common to pay 7-8 USD per standard lot round trip, that is, you pay a total of 7 USD for entering and exiting a position of 100,000 units.

Not only are there different types of brokers but the charts they offer are different as well. Since this is a 24 hour market there is a lot of leeway in determining what the opening and closing times are. A broker in Sydney might consider 5PM their time to be the day's close but that puts us right in the middle of the London session. This has huge impact on traders who are looking to trade candlestick patterns or price action bars. This isn't a recommendation as much as a do-it-or-else. Choose brokers which offer "New York close" charts that is charts which reflect the close of the New York markets as the official daily close. This puts you in sync with the professional traders and big players who you want to be aligned with as much as possible. Doing anything else is simply planning on giving your money away.

The order units or position size is different in FX as compared to stocks. FX units are measured in lots. A standard lot is equal to 100,000 units of currency. A mini lot is 10,000 units and a micro lot is 1000 units and a nano lot is 100 units.

When ordering via most broker platforms, you will abbreviate the standard lot size to 1, mini to 0.1 and micro to 0.01. For example a buy order of 1.30 EUR/USD is equivalent to 1 standard lot and 3 mini lots or in other words 130,000 units of EUR/USD. To spell it out completely, you're selling 130,000 USD for EUR at the ask price quoted to you by the broker. If that seems like a lot of money, don't fret. You can still participate due to the leverage offered in FX.

The price we see on screen for a currency pair is essentially the exchange rate between those currencies. So if you see a price of 149.71 for the GBP/JPY, you will read that as "1 pound is equivalent to 149.71 Yen". Similarly a quote of 0.93817 on the USD/CHF is interpreted as 1 USD is worth 0.93817 Swiss Francs or to put it in even more lay terms, if you exchange 1 USD for Swiss francs you get 0.93817 Swiss francs back. As you can imagine, currency exchange rates don't move much at all. In fact, they usually move less than a cent per session. This is why it is necessary to utilize leverage in the FX market since the price movements are minuscule. This of course, increases the downside risk as well.

A leverage of 1:100 is the most commonly offered level but in the US, brokers are restricted to offering 1:50. That is if you buy a standard lot of USD, 100,000 USD, with 1:100 leverage, you need to post 1000 USD as margin in your account. Many brokers tout leverage offers of up to 1:500 but a beginner should stay away from these levels since things can go south very fast even with 1:100, let alone 1:500. This makes risk management even more critical than it is in the stock markets and indeed, it is precisely a lack of risk management that dooms more traders to failure than an inadequate strategy.

Another feature of the FX market you will need to understand is the swap or carry rate. When you trade a currency pair, say you're long USD/JPY, in actuality you're effectively going long the USD and shorting the JPY. When you carry the position overnight, i.e, past the 24 hour close period for that day, your broker will charge or credit you an amount of interest that is based on the central bank rates prevalent for that currency. So in the previous example, if the Fed has set the short term cash rates at say 2% and the Bank of Japan has set it at say 1%, your broker will pay you a small sum based on your position size overnight since you own the currency with the higher interest rate. If you were short of the USD/JPY, your broker will debit a certain amount. The actual mechanics behind this is beyond the scope of this book since it isn't of more than academic interest.

As you can guess, the amounts debited are usually greater than amounts credited. This is because, the broker themselves need to pay their liquidity providers and when they need to pay, the cost is simply passed onto you. When a credit is received though, most of it is magically pocketed. Those of you who have followed the FX market and trading in general may have heard of the famous "carry trade" strategy. The overnight swap is at the crux of that strategy and it was extremely profitable early last decade due to the wide disparity between the rates of the Greenspan led Fed and the BOJ which was close to 0% rates due to the constant slowdown of the Japanese economy. Current market conditions do not favor this strategy since almost all rates around the world are very close to each other with Europe experiencing unprecedented negative interest rates. If there does arise a similar situation though, the FX market beckons with a ready made strategy. (As a side note: A lot of amateurs refer to a long position in the

USD/JPY as a Yen carry trade by default. Hopefully you understand their mistake now)

Profit and loss calculations are also complicated as compared to the stock market since we need to translate amounts between currencies. In this day and age though, I feel its best to simply use an online calculator or program for your position sizing and P/L calculations instead of relying on pen and paper or even excel. Those who are curious about learning the exact calculations can easily search online for examples. I won't detail these calculations since, to me, they are of nothing more than academic interest and don't add or subtract from your ability to trade.

The FX market is subject to influence from many events. The 24 hour nature of this market means events well past your bedtime have great impact on your open positions. I will elaborate on how this can be managed in the risk management section, but for now it is important for you to know which events you ought to be aware of. You'll find a lot of authorities listing out everything from ISM numbers to European ZEW surveys etc. In reality, just be aware of the ones listed below:

1) Any central bank interest rate/policy announcements and the subsequent press conferences.

2) Non Farm Payrolls- A US economic release which usually occurs on a Friday.

3) Any speeches or press conferences hosted by the chairs of the central banks.

4) Any important ongoing events. For example: Brexit and its earlier cousin, Grexit etc.

5) Any release of FOMC or European minutes of meeting with regards to central bank policy rates.

6) Any major political events like elections or a vote on major issues like Brexit.

The FX market is especially sensitive to these events and some pairs these days barely go anywhere until an event hits. No market more readily lays bare its evolution than FX. A trader has to always be on the lookout over the long term characteristics of the pairs they trade and how is has been changing. The instruments you will trade, over a long period of time, will change around a lot because of this. Another feature to keep track of is correlation and its degree of change.

Correlation refers to the degree of similarity between currency pairs. You will often find, over the long term, certain currencies like the pound and the euro are largely correlated, with the pound being more volatile than the euro. Similarly, the GBP/JPY is closely correlated with the GBP/USD as opposed to the USD/JPY and this means if you're quite good at trading the GBP/USD, chances are you can trade the GBP/JPY as well. While I do not recommend basing a strategy entirely on correlation, since you never know when it'll change, there are successful traders who observe this and take advantage of this. Knowing and observing the relationship between pairs is useful though since some pairs may start moving ahead of others and serve as a warning signal. I'm not listing out any correlations here since they change and as I mentioned, I'm not a fan of basing a strategy around this phenomenon. Indeed, you can be successful even ignoring it completely but it helps to have a well rounded view of the markets you're trading.

A plus point with regards to FX brokers is all of them offer demo or paper accounts for you to practice before going live. Every beginner needs to start trading on a demo account before risking actual money. You'd think this is obvious but many a beginner, in the initial rush of having found a workable strategy, forgets this and lets greed take over. Don't be that person. Conduct your research and limit yourself only to STP brokers in the beginning. Practice your strategy until you know it inside and out and only then risk actual money.

Now that we're done looking at the mechanics of the forex market, lets dive into some basic skills you must master if you want to ever make any money in this market. Please note: the following chapters are very dense and it is recommended you read them multiple times until you can spot what it is I'm talking about on a live chart. Without further ado, lets jump in.

Chapter 3: The Basics- Trends and Ranges

"The trend is your friend", "Always trade with the trend", "Always take the path of least resistance". These are some home truths always spewed by the trading "authorities" everywhere. While these statements have their origin in fact, most of these authorities conveniently forget to mention the most basic of questions: What is a trend and how do I identify the direction?

You've probably read some variation of this piece of advice in answer to that question: "Well just look left to right in the chart! Is it going up? Then you're in an uptrend! Down? You're in a downtrend! Simple!". If there was a prize awarded for the most useless pieces of advice ever given, this one would be right up there with "Yes, its a great idea to meddle with Middle Eastern politics."

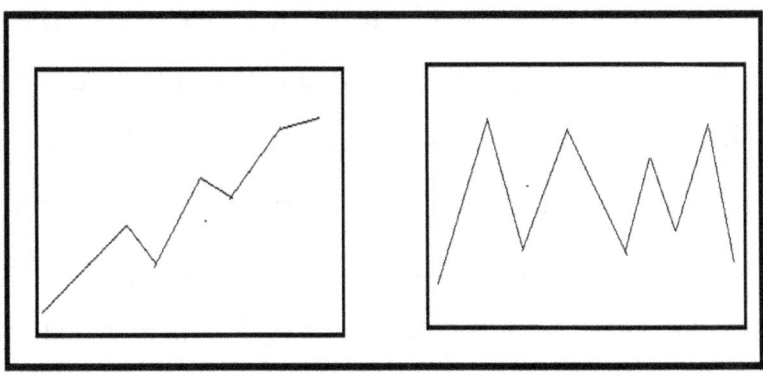

Figure 1: Look, a trend on the left and a range on the right! How simple is this? If only real world charts were this easy

Now don't misunderstand me. These statements have some truth to them but they completely neglect to mention something that is critical to your success in the markets: *The strength of the trend.* Its easy to look left to right on a chart and say if the chart is moving up, down or sideways. However, just because the last bar on the extreme right happens to be higher than the first bar on the left, doesn't mean price is in an uptrend. Trends are more nuanced than that and this is what trend strength uncovers.

What do I mean by trend strength? Simply put, its the degree to which order flow is tilted in favor of a given direction. You will always find trends which have some degree of imbalance between the bulls and bears. Order flow which is completely tilted towards the bulls results in a trend which is extremely bullish. Similarly, order flow which is completely tilted towards the bears will result in a trend which is extremely bearish. The majority of the time, order flow is distributed in some proportion between bulls and bears. Understanding the proportion is key to successful trading.

It follows from the above paragraph that order flow which is equally divided results in a range. In other words, a range is the result completely balanced order flow. This is where the market goes sideways and there isn't any apparent direction. For a market to have direction, there needs to be an imbalance in the order flow.

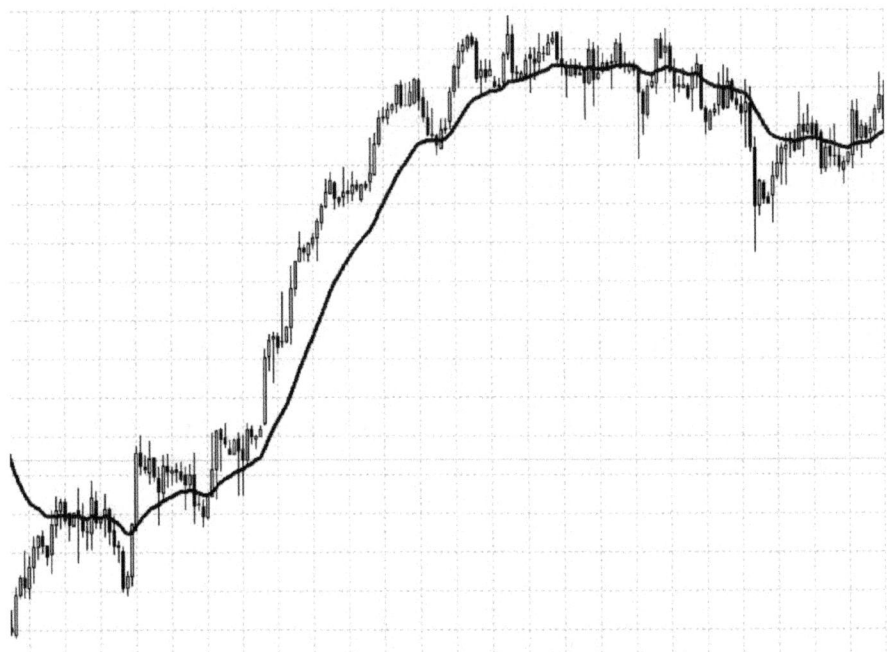

Figure 2: A great example of trend strength changing. Note the size of the bearish bars compared to the bullish ones on the left of the chart and notice how the bullish bars steadily increase compared to the bearish ones in both size and number. Observe the number of full bodies bullish bars compared to the bearish ones. In the middle of the picture, there's a complete lack of bearish bars and bullish trend strength is very high. As we move to the right, the bears re enter and the picture gets flipped as compared to the left. It is now the bears who are exerting greater pressure and the order flow becomes more balanced and tilted towards the bears despite price continuing to be in an uptrend. The trend strength here is very low for obvious reasons.

Now that we've defined what is meant by the strength of a trend, what are some ways we can assess it? Well, since trends are a result of order flow imbalances, it follows that the percentage of bearish orders versus bullish orders will give us the degree to which the market is imbalanced. Thankfully, due to the advent of charts we can do this visually. The following list is a brief method of identifying trend strength:

1) Is price going up or down when seen left to right?

2) What is the proportion of bull candles to bear candles? (or bars if you're so inclined)

3) How frequent are the bullish and bearish candles?

4) What is size of the bullish versus the bearish candles?

5) How much do the bear candles push back into the bull candles and vice versa?

It is important to understand that the above is a qualitative checklist, that is, do not attach numbers to it. For example, it is not more significant that there were previously 5 bullish bars of 6 points average length versus 4 bars of 7 points average length. Looking at it like this is missing the forest for the trees. Your objective should be to get a feel for which way the market is tilted and whether to anticipate a probable continuation of trend or reversal. If trend continuation is probable, ask yourself, how forceful is it and how deep are the countertrend players pushing back?

Sometimes, the degree of pushback into the trend will be huge. Such an occurrence gives us an indication that the trend might be about to flip over to the other side. If you've ever wondered which side of the market to trade, you will appreciate the significance of that statement. Now, not all charts will be simple or clear to you especially if you're starting out. This is where chart time and experience comes in. Clarity in this regards is simply a function of the number of hours you spend analyzing a chart. The more you practice this skill, the easier it becomes. In case the chart on a particular timeframe is unclear, my advice is to simply go up one timeframe. So for example if the 60 minute chart seems muddled, switch to a 4 hour chart and so on. Another indicator which often helps with this is the 20 bar exponential moving average.

The 20 EMA is useful not because 20 is a magic number. It is useful because a large majority of traders use it. Please note though that the 20 EMA is a tool and not a crutch. You should avoid using it as a sole indicator except in a very special case as explained later. If the picture is muddled, the position of price in relation to the 20 EMA will clear things up, that is, if its above or below it. So to re-iterate, the visual way where we look at the frequency and size and pushback of the bars is the best way. You can however take the help of the higher timeframe and 20 EMA sometimes.

Markets will often go sideways, that is, the order flow will be completely balanced. Such situations are referred to as ranges and its tempting to think of them as directionless. Some traders will even use this to justify trading both sides of a range, that is, going long and short. This is a bad idea for a beginner to do, in my opinion, since it is almost certain that a beginner will apply this logic in a formulaic way. The reality is far more nuanced than this.

While the range itself indicates balanced order flow, one must keep in mind that the order flow is balanced for that particular timeframe. The higher timeframe, which will always trump the lower one, may be indicating something entirely different.

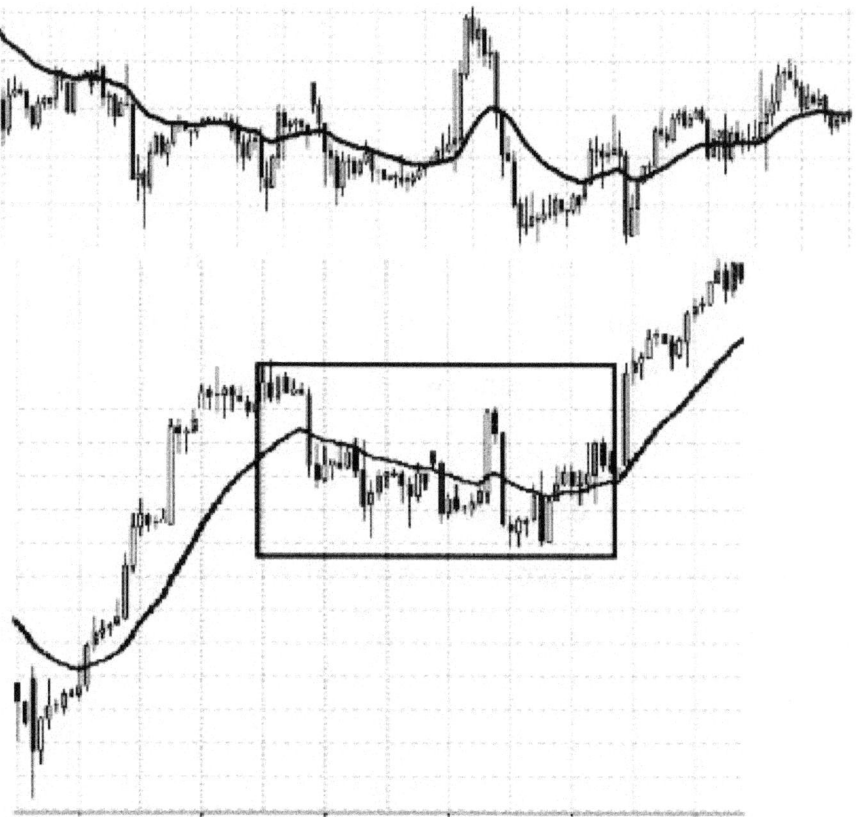

Figure 3: Timeframes matter. The picture on the top depicts a range on the 1 hour timeframe for the DAX. You'd think you can play both sides. However, looking the higher timeframe, the 4 hour chart at the bottom, its obvious the DAX is in an uptrend.
Taking a short is simply going against the odds or the line of least resistance or whatever you want to call it.

In such situations its important to recognize the following: The current timeframe may be indicating one thing but the higher timeframe indicates the exact opposite. There is no contradiction here. The markets are a chaotic place and this often happens. You understanding that there is no conflict here has major implications for our understanding of trading with trends.

Trend trading is more than just looking left to right and blindly determining the direction and placing a trade. We need to also take into account what the higher timeframe is indicating. If the 5 minute indicates a bull trend and the 15 minute indicates a bear trend, placing a buy order (long) on the 5 minute makes that order a countertrend order. Re read that again and let it sink in. Chances are you've never read it before.

Thus far we have seen how we can identify how strong a trend is and how we can anticipate when a reversal is in the offing. I've already mentioned how merely looking left to right isn't the only way to determine a trend and that sometimes a trend will have flipped before the visual-left-right way reveals it. So how do we know when the trend has flipped and that we ought to change our bias to be in line with this? Well, this is what is addressed in the next chapter.

Chapter 4:
Turning Points

The previous chapter was about identifying trends and how the underlying order flow indicates what direction the market is headed in. However, all things come to an end. Successful trading requires us to be able to identify in advance when a trend might be coming to an end so as to enable us to switch sides in the market. Not having this skill will leave us trading the wrong side of the market and no amount of hard work will ensure success in such a scenario.

Its important to remember before we proceed that the markets are chaotic and it doesn't make sense to expect a clean and clear signal. This "Holy Grail" approach to things is what dooms most beginners and causes them to chase that perfect indicator or pattern or setup. The reality is no such thing exists. Even when evaluating trends and the general pattern of the market, you must keep in mind, we aren't trying to unlock some secret code. We're merely trying to get a good idea of which way order flow is headed. If we cannot figure this out with clarity, it makes no sense to participate in the market at that given moment.

The strength of the trend, as explained in the previous chapter, gives us an idea of how many buyers and sellers are present at a given time. Now, when a trend starts to reverse , the number of counter trend players increase. This translates as more counter trend bars on the price chart and hence, a more balanced order flow i.e an equal number of bulls and bears. Eventually, the counter players overwhelm the incumbent trend players and then the trend reverses.

This doesn't mean that every trend is followed by a range and that range is followed by a reversal. That is too simplistic a view for a chaotic environment. However, this holds largely true across all instruments and environments and markets. Remember though, while the order flow may have reversed on a lower timeframe, the higher timeframe may indicate the opposite. That is, you could see a bear trend start on the 5 minute chart but the 15 minute chart still shows a range. Trading such environments, where the lower and higher timeframes don't agree with one another, is something that depends on your level of experience in the markets. I recommend beginners only trade with trend and in line with the higher timeframe. As a rule of thumb, if the higher timeframe is neutral, that is sideways, you can go both long or short with the lower timeframe trend. If the higher timeframe has a direction then only trade in that direction in the lower timeframe.

So now, we can reasonably spot the possible end of a trend before it actually does using the trend strength approach. It is necessary though to draw a line in the sand and designate an area on the chart beyond which, we will know for certain that the trend has reversed. This is because while the order flow may indicate something, an unforeseen event may cause the existing trend to continue. Or simply put, we might be incorrect in our reading of the market.

This line in the sand is essentially a turning point where we flip our bias on the market and start trading the other side in earnest. It is saying "If price goes below XX, I'm switching my bias to bearish from bullish and will go short below that level and remain long above it." So what do these turning points look like on a chart? The most common types are swing highs or lows, a prior range or a level which is present (as a range or swing point) on both the current and higher timeframe.

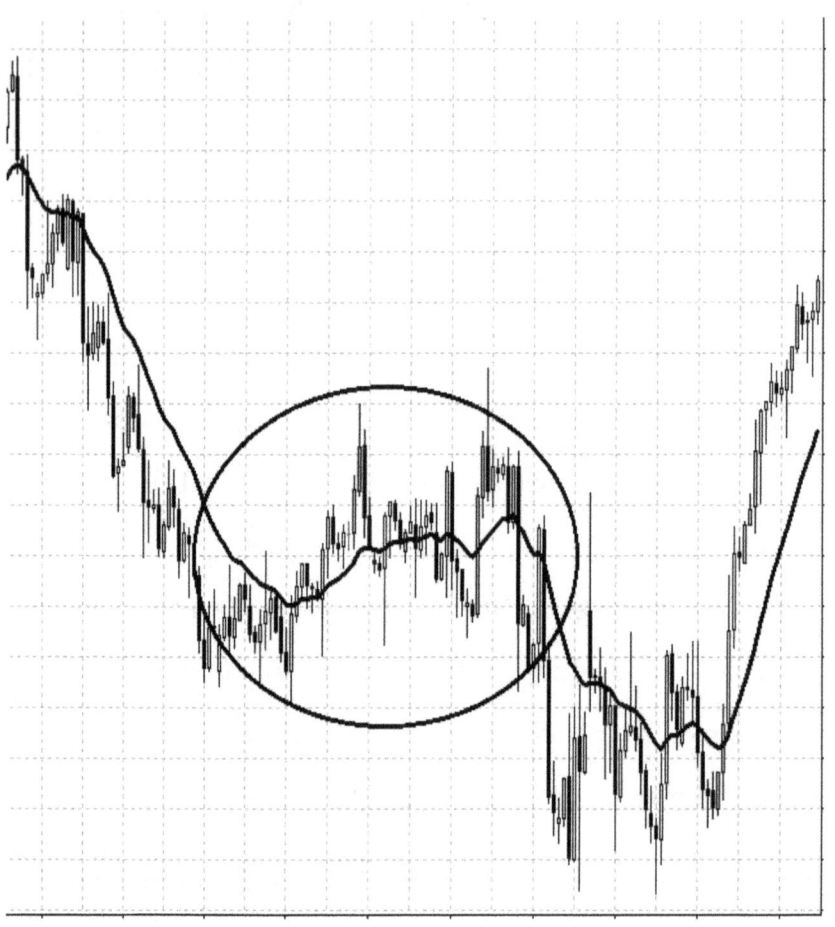

Figure 4: Compare the nature of the buying before versus after and inside the circle. The bullish bars are more frequent and larger in size indicating increasing buying interest. Price ultimately reverses and is in a full fledged bull trend once it clears the prior highs within the circle.

It is important to distinguish an ordinary swing level versus a key swing level to designate as a turning point. In Figure 4, we can see a range before price ultimately reverses but designating the top of this range as a turning point would be incorrect. This is because prior to this, we had a bigger range, denoted by the circle, where buyers showed up in big numbers and were rejected strongly by the sellers. It stands to reason that this level is a well defended one. Therefore, if the buyers can break through this level, the sellers will most likely wave a white flag. Hence, we designate the top of the prior range as the turning point.

Such a reading of the market takes time to build up to and a lot of practice. The rewards are huge though. More than any indicator, this is what will guide you towards the correct direction of trends and ultimately, the correct side of the market to be trading with. Using the example of figure 4, taking a long position within the area highlighted in the circle makes no sense since the trend is bearish. You can make a profit taking a long off the bottom of that range but compare the distance the bullish bars travel versus the distance the bearish bars go. Its obvious which direction has the greater odds of success and higher profit potential.

You will need to extensively practice these basic skills until they become second nature. It is on this bedrock that you will build all of your strategies and indeed, any strategy is useless unless you understand these skills inside out. Let's now move on to some basic strategies you can use to make money in the FX markets.

Chapter 5:
The MACD- Improved

I can hear the groans from all of you. You were promised a new and successful way of trading and here I am introducing the most tired, cliched and common indicator of them all: The MACD. There will be some readers who are unaware of this however, and the next paragraph is for their benefit. Those aware of what this is can safely skip the next one.

The MACD stands for Moving Average Convergence Divergence. It is most commonly pronounced "Mack D" although there are some who pronounce the individual letters out. Briefly, the MACD is a plot which uses 2 moving averages as the input (say the 5 EMA and 20 EMA- designated faster average and slower average) and indicates whether the faster average is above or below the slower average. If its above, the MACD line will have a positive value and negative if below. The idea is, when price starts to rise or fall, the faster, more sensitive average will react first and if it crosses the slower average, it means price is higher/lower than its recent past.

The moment the MACD crosses the 0 level is when the faster average crosses the slower one. General opinion is you go long when it crosses 0 to positive value and short when it crosses 0 to negative value.

The conventional way of using the MACD causes a bunch of false signals since it completely focuses on the value of the averages itself without taking into account prevailing market conditions. Not to mention the fact that since everyone and their grandma knows what the MACD is and they're all using it the exact same way, the effectiveness of using this as a strategy fades. This improved strategy however takes into account the basics illustrated in the previous chapters, namely, trend strength and turning points.

The biggest pitfall everyone falls into in using the MACD is turning it into a quest to determine the ideal numbers for the fast and slow moving averages. When this fails to yield results, people turn to the histogram and try to unlock it as if it contains ancient secrets. There is no secret! Its all right there in front of you on the chart! Not realizing this and applying the old way is a surefire way to insanity. Start embracing the new way right now.

Briefly, here are the rules:

1) Determine trend direction looking left to right and marking any turning points.

2) Determine trend strength. You may use a number or have some grade for it or not. The idea is you understand the degree of strength in the direction.

3) Use any faster and slower EMA number in the indicator input. The actual numbers don't matter so long as there's a decent gap between them. Example: 5 and 20.

4) The MACD will cross 0 before price reaches your turning point. The bar after it closes above/below your turning point, enter in that direction at the close of the bar/candle.

5) If price is already past a turning point and in a well established trend, check to see if the MACD is below/above 0 and that it is confirming the direction of entry. That is, if price is below a turning point and a bear trend is on, enter only when the MACD is below 0 and price remains below the turning point.

6) Place your stop based on trend strength. If trend strength is low, that is, there are substantial counter trend players, place your stop above/below a deep support/resistance level. If trend strength is high, place it above/below a closer level.

7) Place your reward at the same distance as your entry is from your stop level after taking into account commissions if trend strength is low. If strength is high, place it at 2X distance. (For example: If stop is at 2 points from entry and trend strength is low, place the take profit order at 2 points from entry. If trend strength is high, place it at 4 points from entry)

8) Do not use MACD if price is in a range. Just do not.

Alternatively, in case trend strength is low, you can opt to wait for a pullback into a deep support/resistance level and enter close to the level. This enables you to have a closer stop and a potentially larger reward target of 3X. The drawback of course is that you might not enter the trade at all since there's no guarantee that price will pull back. It depends on how aggressive you want to be. My advice is to experiment with both ways on a trial account and see which one suits you best. Only then implement this live.

Please understand this is not a 100% guaranteed winning strategy. This is merely an entry signal. Your actual profits depend on your entry, stop loss and your reward points. It also depends on your ability to pull the trigger and see the trade through to the end. Lastly, it also depends on how much work you're willing to put in to work on the basics. The charts in the next few pages illustrate the method. There's a lot of material that's been packed into a few words in this chapter. Take your time to understand it and be patient with it.

Figure 5: As price crosses the turning point on the FTSE (indicated by the arrow), we see the MACD value is already negative. Trend strength being pretty strong (notice the lack of bullish bars as it approaches the turning point and how the number of bullish bars are decreasing), we can safely place our stop slightly above the broken turning point level. A maximum reward of 2.5 was available speaking conservatively before price turned back into the level.

Note how at the 2nd arrow, a false long signal is generated. Such signals will occur and are unavoidable. They are the cost of doing business.

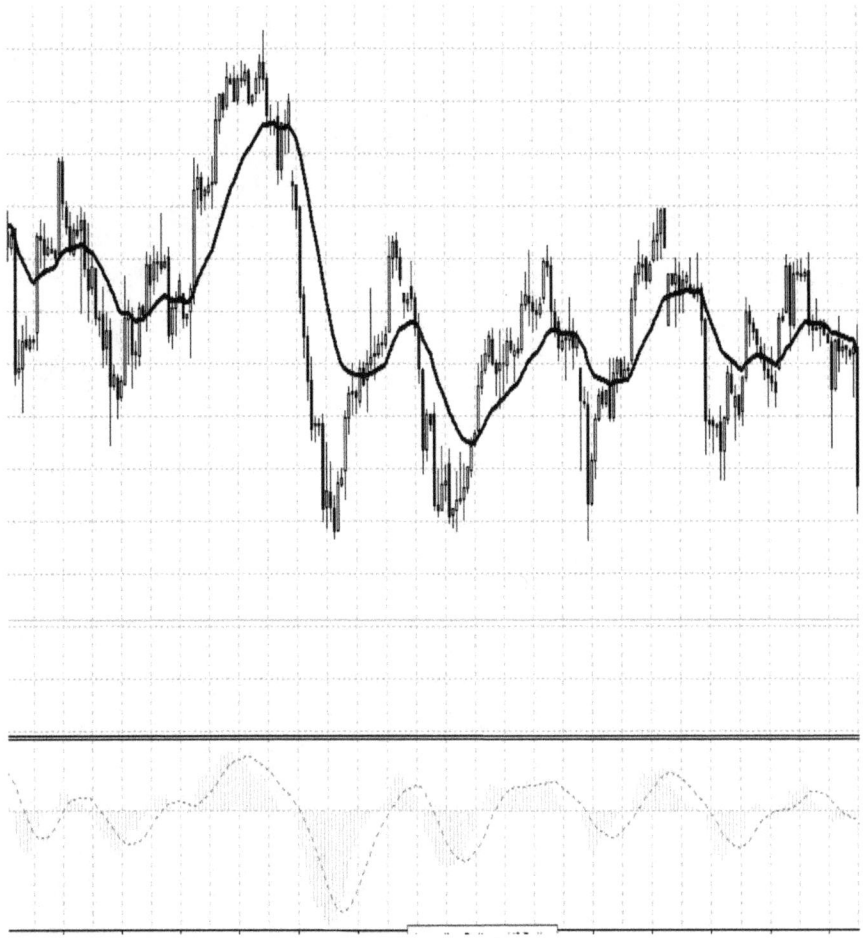

Figure 6: Do not use the MACD in a range. Note the number of times the MACD crosses and re-crosses zero. The number of false signals in incalculable.
Also, since there is no definite trend, there isn't any question of using the MACD to even begin with.

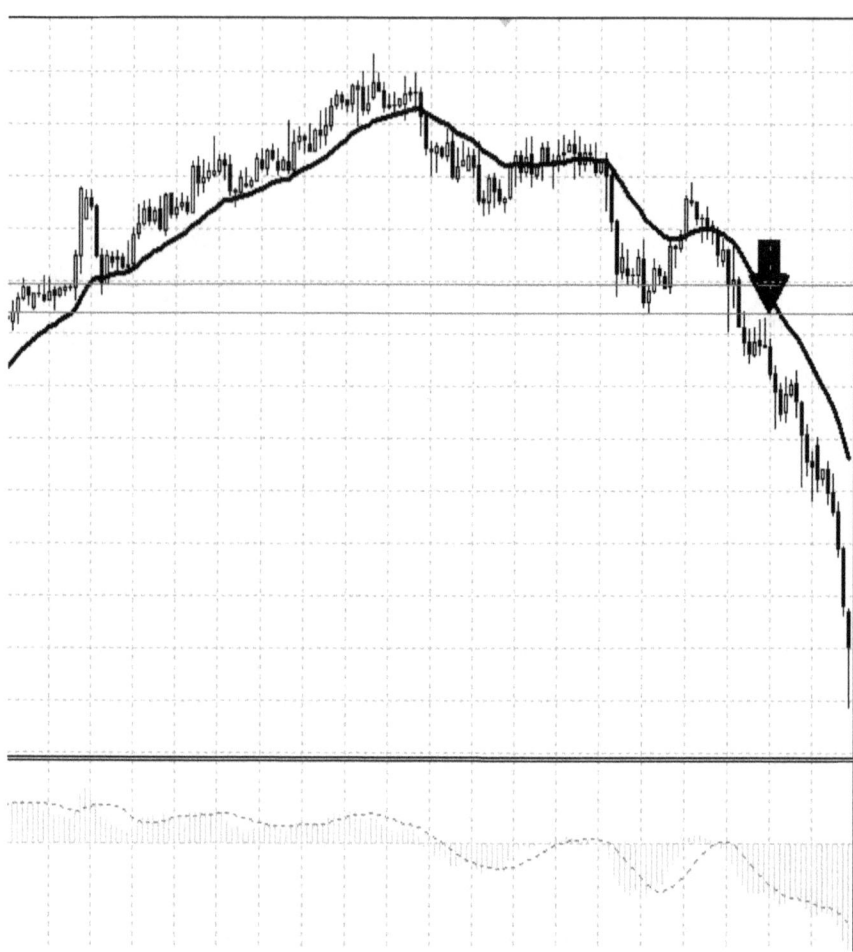

Figure 7: Trend strength will change sometimes and this may cause you to miss entries. Here, after initially showing strong buyer interest prior to the break below the turning point, one might have been tempted to wait for a deeper pullback entry. However, the pullback never materialized.
Decide how aggressive you want to be and trial it first. Implement whichever approach suits you best.

Chapter 6:
20 EMA S/R

As mentioned previously, the 20 EMA is one of the indicators we use to sometimes help determine trend direction. The only reason this is an important indicator is because of the sheer number of traders, both amateur and professional, who implement this as a part of their strategies. The number 20 by itself is not a holy grail and has no real significance.

Often, the 20 EMA ends up behaving as dynamic support or resistance (S/R). This is often the case in trends which have a high degree of trend strength. When trends are heavily imbalanced it doesn't take much to get with trend players on board and the closest S/R often acts as a trend continuation zone. The problem with using the closest static S/R is that different people have different views with regards to the strength of levels on a chart.

Therefore the solution is to use something which everyone agrees on. This is where the 20 EMA is useful. Like a self fulfilling prophecy, its usefulness stems from the fact that everyone thinks its useful. Might sound a bit dodgy but then again, if you think about it, all forms of price and money work on the same principle.

Executing this strategy requires you to have a very strong ability to identify trend strength. Again, this only comes about as a result of practice. This strategy is a prime example of how mastering the basics, instead of jumping between systems recklessly, is what gives you the big rewards. Also note the simplicity of the system. There's no need to fill your chart space with a ton of indicators or keep staring at the screen endlessly.

Simply assess trend strength and enter close to the 20 EMA as price approaches it. Place your stop below the 20 EMA. The exact location is more of an art than science and is something one must practice on a trial account. Again, you can be aggressive and get real close or be conservative and place your stop a fair distance away. A good rule of thumb is to look at the extent to which the 20 EMA was punctured previously and place your stop at the same distance below the EMA.

Needless to say this strategy does not work in a range or in a trend with low or even medium trend strength. The best way to implement this is to practice on a trial account and develop a feel for it and only then implement it with a live account. Aim for at least a 2X reward with this strategy.

Figure 8: Trend strength is very high with hardly any countertrend players involved. Note how the FTSE constantly bounces off the 20 EMA.

As trend strength decreases, it hangs around longer near the 20 EMA but still doesn't go below it considerably.

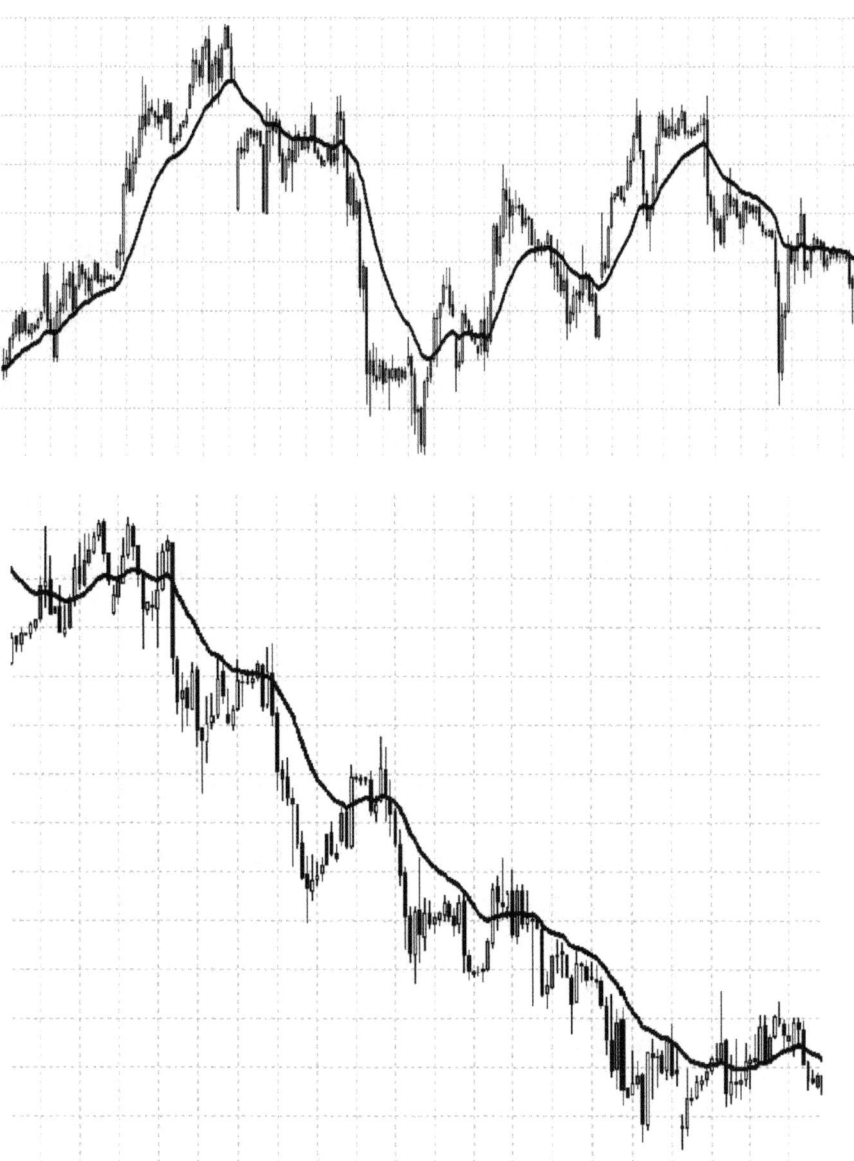

Figure 9: This does not happen in the case of a range (above) or in a trend with medium trend strength (below). The point is to understand the basics and then implement strategies.
Blind application only results in losses!

Chapter 7: Momentum Patterns

Almost everyone who has dabbled in trading knows and has some experience with patterns. Patterns come in all shapes and sizes and some indeed can be absurd to consider. The truth is all patterns are highly subjective and depend on the trader themselves. Trading is part art and part science. Pattern recognition comes firmly under the artsy part of trading.

If you feel you're more of a visual person then pattern recognition trading might be the way to go. There are a lot of crazy patterns out there but you need to focus on only a few tried and tested ones. These are listed below and we'll take a look at them individually.

1) Cup and Handle

2) Head and Shoulder

3) Ascending triangle

4) Descending triangle

5) Parabolic curve

Trading big moves is specifically about volatility. The greater the volatility in the markets the greater the chances are of making money. The key to making good money in the FX markets while trading is to identify pairs which are making great headway. After all, no one wants to be long of some instrument that isn't headed anywhere while the rest of the market is going up 10% or more. The above patterns not only help identify momentum in stock but also generate reliable entry signals. The general rule of thumb with trading patterns is to aim for a reward of 2X risk.

Cup and Handle

The trend strength is a vital aspect of all the patterns we will be discussing in this chapter. The Cup and Handle pattern is called so due to its visual similarity with an actual cup with a handle. This pattern is a great indicator of a potential breakout and a trend reversal. Applying it though requires nuance and a lot of traders apply this blindly without any thought.

This is true of all patterns since most traders forget that successful trading isn't about the ability to draw the prettiest picture on your chart. Its about understanding what's going on behind the scenes that results in the charts we see. This behind the scenes action is clearly decoded using the trend strength approach. Let us consider the shape of the cup and handle. The curved part of this pattern, that is, the cup, occurs because price is going largely sideways and trend strength is low. The handle part of the pattern indicates lower with trend players and increased counter trend strength. In low trend strength environments, as mentioned previously, we always need to be on the lookout for a reversal. It is very important you understand what is being implied here. The pattern is a good indicator because of the underlying price and trend mechanics NOT because it is a magical shape that by itself pushes price upwards.

The Cup and Handle is best used in environments with low trend strength. The pattern is most powerful when the top of the cup is an important level across timeframes and functions as a turning point. The least optimal use of this pattern is as a trend continuation signal, that is, in a range that occurs in an established trend. The reason for this is because the pattern is a great reversal signal and reversals tend to occur as the strength of the counter trend players steadily increases. In a strong trend strength environment, it doesn't make sense to look for reversals.

This is why most traders fail at implementing patterns of any kind. Blindly implementing them without taking into consideration trend mechanics is as useful as drawing random shapes on a chart. The Cup and Handle when implemented correctly is a very powerful signal and trades entered using this pattern tend to have a large reward compared to risk. You can enter based on how aggressive you want to be. Entering prior to the breakout with a stop near the middle of the range is a pretty aggressive approach but has the highest reward to risk ratio. There is a greater chance of failure however. Entering after the breakout on a pullback has greater chances of success but you might end up missing the trend altogether if the breakout is powerful.

My personal opinion is to enter on a stop order just past the range high. This way, you might not get the best price fills but atleast you'll be a part of the trend. Aim for atleast a 2X reward on this pattern.

The Cup and Handle is a bullish indicator. The bearish version of this indicator is the reverse cup and handle where the cup is inverted. The shape of the pattern doesn't matter as long as you can understand why the shape gets created in the first place and why it indicates what it does.

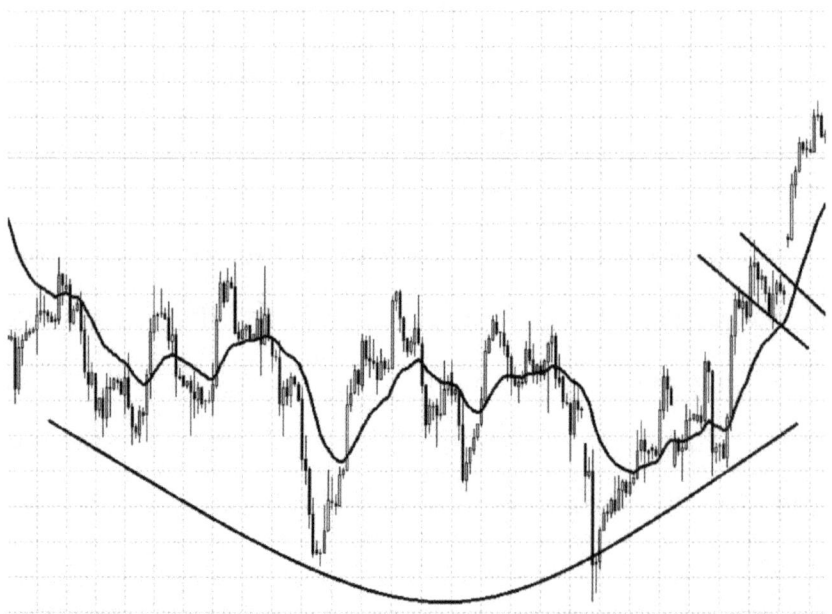

Figure 10: This particular example is an imperfect cup and handle but illustrates how trend strength trumps pretty shapes. Increasing bullish interest helps build the cup shape. The handle is caused by extremly low bearish interest. The level is a turning point given the number of times the bulls were previously rejected around there.
Post the handle, price gaps up the next day and is in a strong bull trend. Your shapes need not be perfect. You understanding of trend strength however does need to be so.

Head and Shoulders

The head and shoulders is perhaps the most quoted and oldest pattern in the history of technical analysis. This is yet another reversal pattern which indicates the end of a bull trend and an impending reversal. The key to using this pattern is to look at the trading volumes on the head versus the shoulders, especially the right shoulder.

The volume should be lower on the bullish bars and greater on the bearish bars on the right shoulder. Again, as with the cup and handle, we see how market mechanics trumps any shape. Lower volumes indicate lower bullish interest and thus causes a reversal. But wait. You'll note I'd previously said volumes in FX cannot be accurate since the market isn't centralized. Well, this is one of those scenarios where the volume is important but isn't as important as you would believe. What is crucial is that we get a snapshot of what's happening. So really even if we only see a fraction of the total volumes, as long as it conforms to what the pattern requires, it is valid. The trend strength anyway gives us a good idea of which way order flow is tilted so the volume not being complete isn't as big a negative as it appears on the surface.

A great optimizer of this pattern is when the base of the structure is a turning point. You can enter on the break of the base or on a pullback into the base. However, this depends on your level of aggressiveness. Aim for atleast a 2X reward with this pattern.

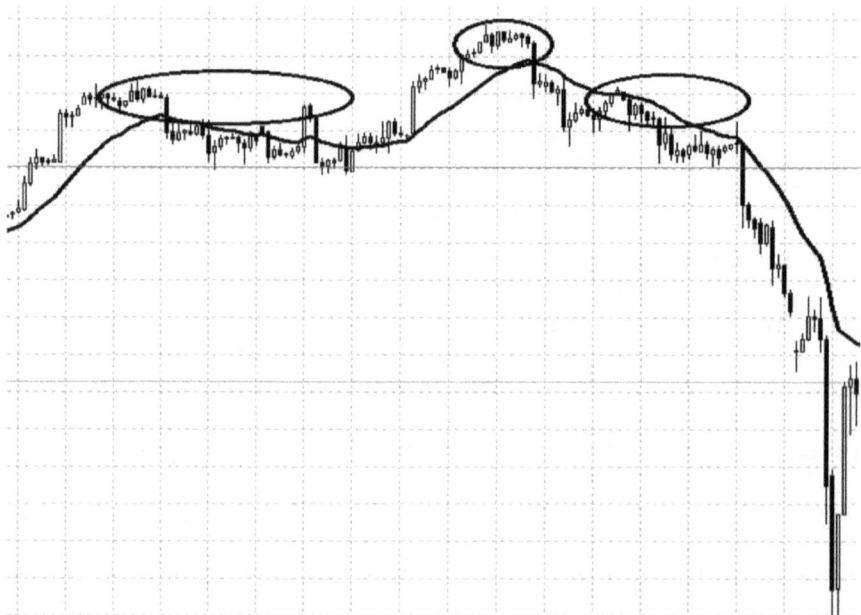

Figure 11: Yet another imperfect shape but if you understand the importance of trend strength, you'll see how significant this pattern is. The 2nd shoulder barely looks like a shoulder but more significantly, the lack of bullish effort speaks volumes. Th subsequent breakout confirms this.

This is a bearish pattern as previously mentioned. The inverse of this is a bullish pattern. Again, don't get caught up too much in the exact shapes and instead understand what causes them in the first place.

Ascending Triangle

This pattern is classified as a continuation pattern as opposed to a reversal pattern like the prior 2 we've looked at. The key point about continuation patterns you need to understand is that you ought to implement them only in medium to strong trend strength environments. Looking for a successful ascending triangle in a low strength environment shows a lack of understanding of how this pattern comes to be in the first place.

In a high strength environment, as price approaches a key resistance level (this pattern applies only to bull trends), the bears push back initially. However, because bullish strength is so high, their efforts eventually peter out and this presents itself as a rising triangle on the chart. A good optimizer of this indicator is to see whether volumes are decreasing on the bearish bars and increasing on the bullish ones. If the volume data is unclear, it isn't a problem since its just an optimizer. The key is to understand the mechanics behind the chart.

Figure 12: The triangle looks imperfect but given the price environment and by gauging the trend strength we realize that the pattern doesn't need to be perfect.
Increasingly lower bearish interest and stronger bullish interest causes price to breakout violently

Again, this pattern works best in a high trend strength environment. There may be isolated cases where it works in a low strength environment but really, you want to put yourself in places where the odds of success are greater.

Understanding the order flow that creates this pattern will make it abundantly clear why a high strength environment gives the best odds for this pattern. My preferred entry is a stop order past the top of the triangle with the stop below the prior low within the triangle. Aim for atleast 2X reward with this pattern.

Descending Triangle

Like its bullish equivalent, the descending triangle is a trend continuation pattern and should not be used to predict reversals. The order flow is reversed in this pattern with the bears repelling the bullish efforts and eventually the bear trend continues as pressure builds. The entry and exit methods are the same as for the ascending triangle.

Figure 13: Trend strength is high in this case and subsequent bullish efforts are overcome by the bears until non existent.
Note how the trend strength changes to a medium strength one right after the breakout. This signals to us that the environment is changing and we should be on the lookout for possible reversal patterns.
Needless to say, it is trend strength which forms the basis of everything

Parabolic Curve

Off all the patterns we're looking at in this book, this is perhaps the riskiest of them all but the potential rewards are significant. Ironically this is actually the easiest pattern to recognize and enter from a technical standpoint. The difficulty arises on a psychological level and it is for this reason that the traders who are the most successful at implementing this pattern are either rank beginners or extremely experienced traders. As such I would not recommend trading this pattern unless you have good awareness of your mindset and it weaknesses and have experience in executing a number of traders until you do not have any fear of pulling the trigger.

This is a reversal pattern and often occurs at the end of a euphoric rise or fall. The euphoria attached to the price movement is what gives rise to the opportunity since the trend becomes unsustainable. A key optimizer of this pattern is the presence of a buying or selling climax (covered in the next chapter). More than anything else this signifies that the trend is overextended. Do not make the mistake however of thinking the climax by itself means the trend is at an end. There has to be a steady increase in the angle of the trend until it becomes almost 90 degrees. Ideally you will want to see atleast 3 changes in the angle of the trend.

The trade entry point for this pattern is more of an art than science. You may choose to enter at the close of the bar which breaks the final trendline or you may choose to wait for a mini pullback into the trendline. As with everything else, the reward risk profile changes with entry. The reward, in my opinion, should be atleast 4X risk to compensate for the low hit rate of this strategy. Generally speaking if you can achieve an accuracy rate of 25-30%, you're doing really well.

This brings me back to the point about how psychologically taxing this strategy is. Not only are we trading against a strong trend, we're actually taking on hysteria. It isn't easy to zag when others zig especially when it seems the entire market is against you. As a trader, you need to always be aware of your weaknesses and how they manifest and attack you in any given situation. This is never more true than when trading this strategy. A losing streak of 10-15 trades is quite common and you need to educate yourself on the importance of variance and probabilities in any trading strategy.

Most of all, you need to assess whether this strategy is for you or not. Everyone has different risk profiles and it isn't a negative if you're able to execute certain strategies over others. If anything, doing exactly that is what will ensure success in the markets. Always trial a strategy out extensively and start small. Refer to the chapter on risk management and mindset for more on this.

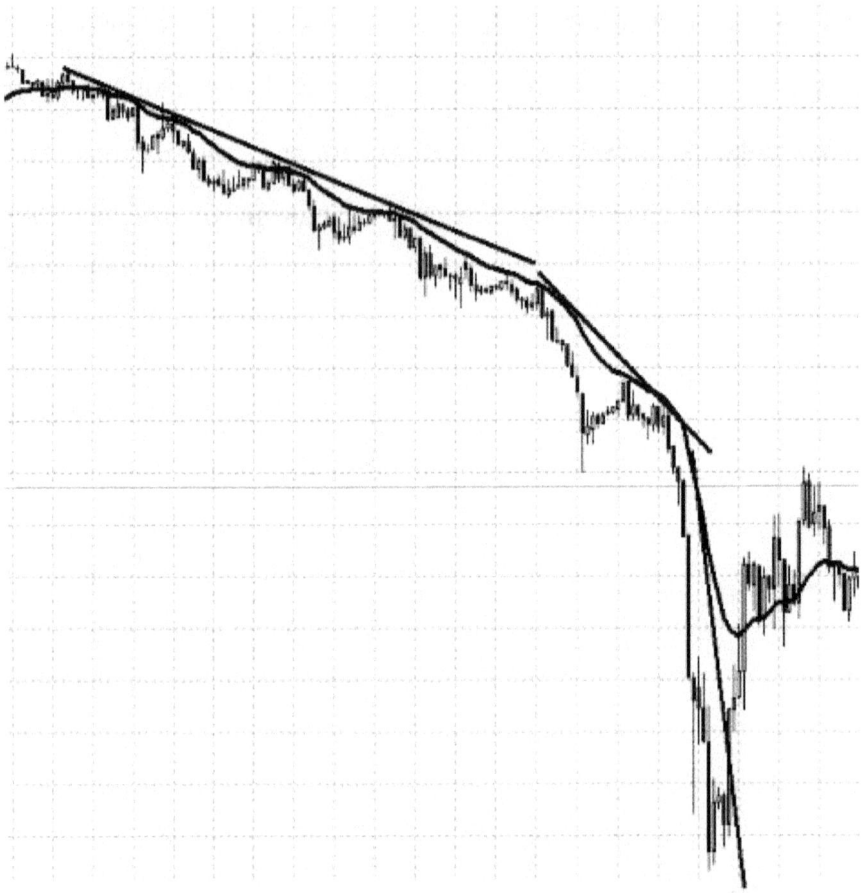

Figure 14: A bearish parabolic arc illustrates both how lucrative and risky this pattern can be. Increasing downside pressure results in a runaway bear trend on the FTSE.
Eventually the trend is unsustainable and a long entry at the break of the last line would have yielded atleast 3X reward speaking conservatively.

Chapter 8:
Price Action Patterns

As a beginner, I do not recommend getting into pure price action since this is a skill that is fairly advanced and rushing into it is a surefire way to confuse yourself. There are some beginner friendly price action methods however which I recommend for their simplicity and ease of application. My personal opinion is that price action is ultimately the only way to successfully trade the markets since by reading price, we're only a step removed from the order flow. Nothing else offers us a closer look in the FX markets since the order book is unavailable.

The 3 main price action patterns you need to be aware of, as a beginner, are:

1) Inside Bars (IB)

2) Pin Bars (PB)

3) 2 Bar Reversal (2B/Revs)

Before we begin, let me re-iterate something which I've already done multiple times. The strategies listed here are of use only if you understand and trade in line with the principles of trend strength. You cannot blindly take, for example, every single IB that presents itself. You need to understand the specific environments in which such patterns work and most of all you must understand this: The patterns are powerful because the underlying price mechanics and order flow create them. They aren't powerful because of their shape or because of how pretty they look. In my experience, most traders understand this intellectually but fail to implement this when trading. You need to start off by determining the trend strength and the price environment (turning points etc) and then start looking for entry signals. The environment determines which signals you look for.

Now that that's clear, lets move on. We will first tackle the inside bar.

Inside Bars

The inside bar is a fairly straight forward pattern to spot. The entire pattern consists of 2 bars, with the bar to the left engulfing the bar to the right. The bar on the right is referred to as an inside bar since it seems to be "inside" the bar to the left. This pattern is best used as a trend continuation indicator, that is, in environments where the trend strength is increasing and the counter trend players are steadily being overwhelmed. An understanding of the price mechanics behind this pattern will give a clearer picture of why this is so.

As trend strength continues to increase and as the market becomes ever more imbalanced to one side, the counter trend players' strength continually diminishes. Eventually it reaches a point where the players on one side of the market are so forceful that all the counter trend players can muster is a cursory effort at repelling the opposite side. This presents itself as a small bar which goes against the trend and is unable to match the bar that preceded it. The with trend order flow is so strong that sometimes the counter trend players fail to even register a single bar in their favor and only manage to slightly halt proceedings.

Such a temporary halt gives us a great indication of where to hop on board the trend and ride it to profits. When looking at this pattern you want the bar on the left to be in the direction of the trend, that is, if we're in a bull trend, the bar on the left should be a bullish one. If a bear trend, then the bar on the left should be a bearish one. The direction of the inside bar, or bar on the right, doesn't matter as long as it satisfies the requirement that its entirety, including any wicks and tails, is confined within the boundaries of the bar on the left.

Remember to use this pattern only in strongly trending environments or in instances where the trend strength is clearly becoming more and more biased towards one side. Another rookie mistake to avoid is to blindly see that a bar has printed inside the one to its left and neglect the trend direction of the previous bar. It needs to be with trend always. There will be times when a bar will be inside the bar on the left but its body will be almost the same size. In these cases, its best to ignore the pattern since it indicates the underlying price mechanics are not favorable. Recall what was said earlier about the order flow creating patterns which are favorable. If you can understand the underlying mechanics, you will understand what optimizes this pattern.

The best way to enter, according to me, is to place a stop order just beyond the bar on the left so you're targeting an entry on the break of the high or low of that bar, in the direction of the trend. An aggressive stop placement would be just past the high or low of the inside bar, depending on the direction of the trade. A more conservative placement would be above the high or low of the bar on the left. Play around with both methods on paper and see which strategy fits you best. When I say fits you, I don't mean which one you're comfortable with, I'm referring to which stop placement makes you more money. Target at least 1.5-2X risk with this pattern. Usually, you'll find price runs a lot further so look at taking a partial exit at a 2X reward and trailing your stop downward thereafter. I don't recommend beginners take partial exits though.

You may read in some places that IBs are a great indicators of reversals as well. While this may have been observed by certain "authorities", in my experience, this is never the case and simply leads to more confusion. Stick to using inside bars as a continuation signal and you'll make more money than most. There's no need to complicate things unnecessarily.

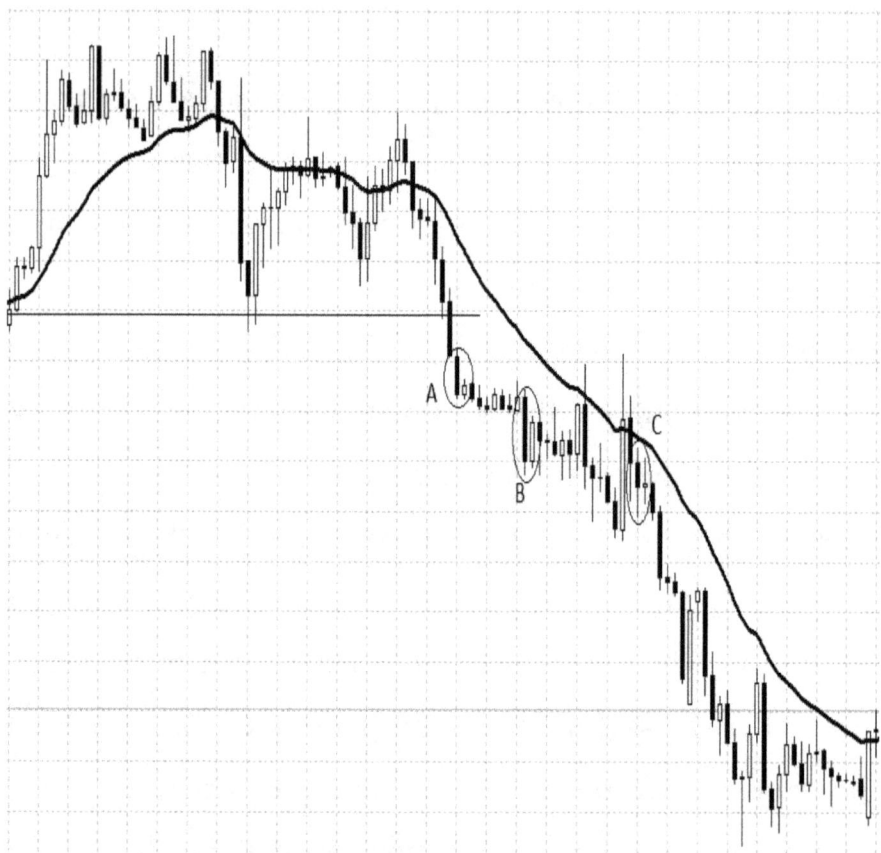

Figure 15: A brief lesson on how to and how not to use the IB pattern. As price breaks out beyond the turning point on the USDSGD, we can see a very strong bearish trend. Bullish participation is negligible.
The first instance of such participation after the break of the turning point comes at "A" where we see a clear IB pattern. Note the characteristics of this particular example. The relative sizes especially and what preceeded the pattern.
Price continues downwards but at B, we receive both an IB and a warning. The size of the IB is relatively bigger and is greater than half of the bar on the left. This particular example has lower odds but you would be justified in taking it.
Subsequent price moves result in a loss for B but our position at A is still in good profit. As bullish participation increases we should have discarded the possibility of finding a good IB pattern by the time we reach C. Compare trend strength, bar size and preceeding action between cases C and A.
This underlines the power of the pattern but more importantly how trend strength determines everything.

Figure 16: An example of an IB cluster here on the 60 minute chart of the GBPJPY. Price is already establishing an environment where bullish strength is decreasing. Prior to this IB cluster, the bulls push back for a while but note the relative distance they manager to travel and the rather pathetic sizes of the bullish bars. The bears reject this emphatically and this cluster represents the last gasp of the bulls who manage just one bullish bar.

Don't let the fact that this is a cluster throw you off. Always keep the trend strength characteristics in mind and the actual pattern second. As long as you're on the right side of the price mechanics, the pattern itself is secondary.

Figure 17: The pattern works across all timeframes because it has the backing of the trend strength approach.
Here on the daily chart of the AUDUSD, see how many instances of the IB pattern you can find.
The prior examples were on the 60 minute and lower timeframes. It doesn't matter what timeframe you're looking at since buying and selling takes place on all levels and leaves a footprint no matter the timeframe.

Pin Bars

The term pin bar refers to a candle which has either a tail at the bottom or a wick at the top. Generally accepted convention is that the body of the pin should be less than a third of the entire length of the bar. I'm not a fan of mathematical boundaries like these since it doesn't make sense to restrict yourself but suffice to say, just look at the bar. If it feels like its a pin visually, go ahead and take it without getting hung up on bar proportion calculations.

It is important to understand what the underlying price mechanics are when it comes to a pin bar. Let's say we're in a price move and as it exhausts itself, the counter trend players start pushing back with increasing strength. The pin bar with a wick represents a case where sellers have started pushing against the bulls and the bar with a tail represents the opposite, that is, the bulls pushing back against the bears. Just like with the inside bar, it is important to realize that the pin bar is a result of underlying price mechanics and isn't a cause of order flow in any direction. So it always pays to analyze the price environment from a trend strength perspective.

Given the preceding description, it should become clear that the pin bar is a reversal indicator. Now here comes the tricky bit. The best way to use this pattern is as a trend continuation one. This will be confusing and those of you who have used and studied pin bars previously from existing "authorities" out there will not have thought of using them in this way. The best way to trade is to trade with the trend, especially if you're a beginner. It doesn't make sense to take the hard route when an easier one is available. So how does one use a reversal pattern to predict a continuation?

Before I elaborate I want to point out something. If you've been paying attention thus far, you'll have noted in the previous chapter, I recommended using the cup and handle pattern purely as a reversal pattern. And here I am, saying use this particular reversal pattern as a continuation one. The reason is this: The cup and handle involves a significant number of price bars and encompasses a lot of order flow within its confines. This gives us a substantial body of work within which we can judge the prevalent conditions and increases our odds of predicting a reversal. A pin bar, in contrast, is merely 1 bar. What makes you think 1 bar is more special than the next one in any market? Even the significance of important event bars diminishes within an hour of their occurrence. So how on earth can one pin bar decide and cement the case for a reversal of a trend which as been running for say 20-30 bars?

This applies to all timeframes and again illustrates how blind application of indicators without understanding order flow results in losses and in traders blaming the pattern when in reality, it is the trader that doesn't understand the nature of the market. Don't be that person who blindly applies indicators expecting some sort of magic solution that unlocks market secrets. The markets are far too chaotic and nuanced for one bar to ever have magical properties.

Having got that out of the way, lets proceed. The key to using this pattern is to understand that all trends have some form of imbalance in them. The degree varies but there are always counter trend players present looking to press their case. No market can exist without the other side. In a high trend strength environment, the counter players hardly get a look in and need to get out of the way quickly. As the steam begins to run out of the with trend players though, the counter players force periods where price goes sideways or maybe even retraces a bit before the with trend players wake up and the push continues. In these sideways movements or pauses, the orders are fairly evenly distributed, even though it may be for a short time and indeed, in some of them, the counter trend players may even have the upper hand for the time being. It is a reversal of this, counter trend, order flow that will indicate when the larger trend is ready to resume and the with trend players are ready to continue onward. It is important for you to understand this so take your time to absorb what has been said here.

A pin bar in such sideways environments or areas where the trend pauses, indicates a reversal of the sideways/counter trend flow and thus a continuation of the larger trend. This is the correct way of using a pin bar pattern. Common wisdom is to specify that pin bars signify reversals and everybody rushes to declare pin bars as the ultimate predictors of a trend which has lost steam. It is a mistake which I have made myself in the past. Your odds of success are extremely low to non existent if you think a single bar can reverse order flow biased towards a particular direction. If you find yourself thinking this way, your understanding of trend strength is inadequate and I recommend more practice with this. Always remember, that these patterns are simply to help with our entry timing. They do not dictate or cause any order flow by themselves.

An entry on the close of the pin bar with a stop below or above the wick/tail or closest support/resistance is the best entry method. Aim for at least a 2X reward with this and more advanced traders can take partial exits and trail their stops. The charts on the following pages will illuminate pin bars further.

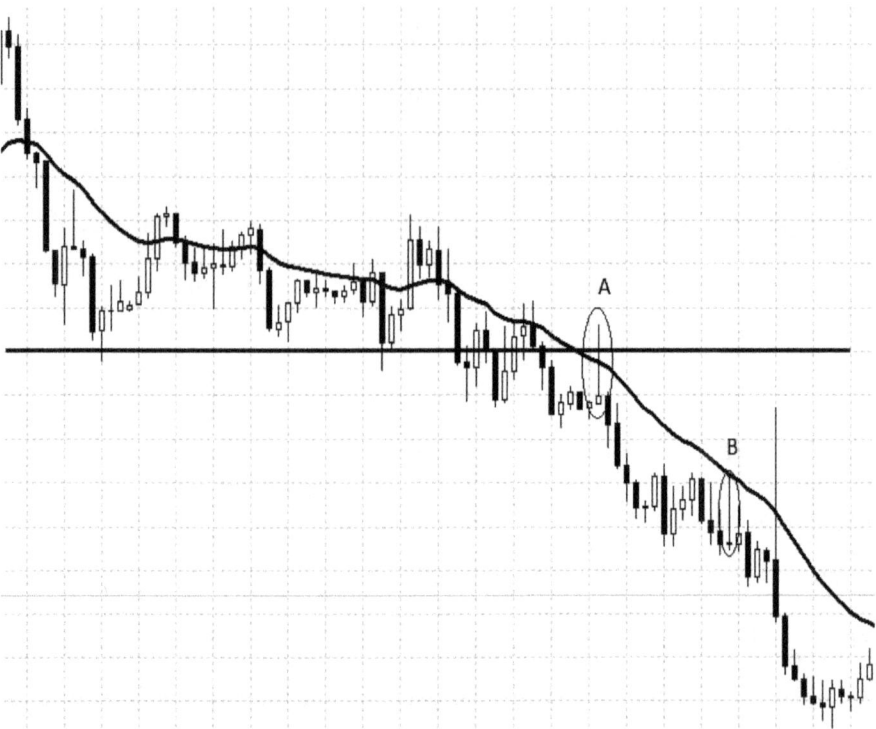

Figure 18: Using a reversal signal as a trend continuation one. Here we see the AUDUSD break below the reversal point with low trend strength and until the pin bar A, price can't seem to make up its mind which way to go. Post the pin bar though we see bullish participation dwindle dramatically and a trend is on.

In the first sideways pattern after A, we see another pin bar B form. Again notice how bullish participation dwindles. This particular signal though would have resulted in a loss thanks to the massive bar caused by an event shortly after. Such things happen in the markets and are the cost of doing business.

An entry from A though gives us a reward of atleast 2X, conservatively, so we're still in good profit. Understand that it is the order flow creates these bars as opposed to thinking a pin bar magically means counter trend players disappear.

Figure 19: The daily chart of the NZDUSD shows a multiple number of pin bars both counter and with trend. This example displays why its ridiculous to apply a in indicator without any consideration for the trend strength and direction. Which pin bars do you think you ought to trade and which ones you ought to leave alone? Its pretty obvious but the answer is at the bottom.

Compare the distance price travels post the counter trend pins and whether your odds of success are greater on that side or on the trending side. By the time pin bar #s 6 and 8 occur, price has been in an uptrend for over a month. How many hours of bullish momentum is that? Ask yourself if one measly bar is enough to overturn all those hours of momentum? Can 1 bar ever be magical enough to do so? This is why we use the pin bar as a continuation pattern, not a trend reversal one.

Answer: Avoid 1,2,3,5,6,8

2 Bar Reversals

2 bar reversals are another powerful reversal pattern which we will use as a continuation one much like the pin bar. The pattern itself is fairly easy to spot and consists of 2 bars which are mirror image of each other. If the bar on the left is a bullish one which closes right near its highs, the bar on the right is a bearish one which closes near its lows. Ideally, we want 2 bars with strong closes, that is, near their highs and lows and no wicks or tails. The term mirror image might confuse some beginners so let's break this down some more.

A 2 bar reversal is, from an order flow perspective, the exact same as a pin bar, except the reversal occurs over 2 bars instead of one. Indeed, if you imagine both the bars as one combined, the result will look like a pin bar. This is the best of way of determining whether or not a couple of bars form this pattern. This might seem tedious at first but with practice, you will be able to automatically spot it. The important thing to understand here is what the pattern tells us about the order flow, instead of looking at it as some sort of magical shape.

Since this is essentially a pin bar, playing out over two bars instead of one, the rules of the pin bar bar apply here as well and this is traded the same way. Aim for atleast a 2X reward with this pattern. The charts on the following pages illustrate this.

Figure 20: The 1 hour chart of the NZDUSD displays atleast two 2 bar reversals which can be used as trend continuation signals.
Notice how when you overlay the bars on top of one another, they form a pin bar. Indeed, the order flow principles are the same and they are traded the same way.

Final Words on PBs and 2B/Revs

While the charts I've displayed here to illustrate how these bars are traded are quite clean and clear, in reality, you will find a large number of pins and 2b/revs being thrown up in the markets. It will be confusing as to which signals you ought to take and which ones to discard. Those of you who have been paying attention would have noticed that I haven't mentioned anything about these signals with respect to trend strength whereas the section on IBs was pretty saturated with it. Well, your wait is over.

The key to picking the best pins and 2b/revs is to look for them in appropriate trend strength environments, when price is moving sideways in a trend. This means we need to look for them in environments with either strong or medium trend strength. Those environments where the counter trend players are clearly becoming stronger, you need to stay away from since the order flow is far too balanced for a couple of bars or one bar to have any significant impact. In other words, we want to look for these signals in environments where price only needs a small provocation to resume the trend it was in. This means, you do not use these signals to predict breakouts.

It should also be evident now why we do not use these as reversal signals since at the point of reversal, order flow is largely balanced.

The demarcation line between a trend which has a strength of medium versus say weak-medium is up to you to determine based on your experience and comfort level. For example, in figure 20 above, you will notice that instance number 2 of the 2b/rev occurred in an environment where it looked like price was about to reverse. I've highlighted this because I personally feel comfortable taking this signal. If you're starting out, this is an advanced entry to take and an intimidating one and I recommend you stay away from such entries until you build up your skills via practice.

Master trend strength and get comfortable with it and you'll see your quality of trades skyrocket.

Chapter 9:
Risk Management

You might be tempted to think we've made it back to the boring part of the book now that the indicator and strategy section is finished. The truth is, along with the basics, this is perhaps the one thing that will ensure your success more than anything else. Consider this: Great risk management can mitigate a mediocre strategy but poor risk management will certainly ruin a great strategy.

If you're familiar with trading and have read multiple books on the subject, chances are most of them boil risk management down to your risk per trade, stop loss and position size etc. The reward risk ratio is often presented as the catch all solution to understanding risk management. The truth is the risk reward ratio of your strategy is merely the starting point. Risk in trading contains both quantitative and qualitative aspects. In this chapter, my aim is to enlighten you on both aspects of this. First, let us look at the quantitative aspect.

Quantitative Risk

Any trading strategy, if it needs to be successful, needs to have an edge. This edge can be measured at it most basic level using 2 key statistics, namely, the reward/risk ratio (hereby referred to as R) and your win rate percentage. Most traders get hung up on either one of these numbers and neglect to understand that these 2 work in tandem. One affects the other. A typical newbie is someone who aspires to a 100% win rate and a 5R+ ratio. This is some Alice in Wonderland level of thinking and is practically impossible.

The more realistic way of approaching this is to first of all determine, given your R per trade, what is the minimum win rate you need to breakeven? Notice I said breakeven, not make millions. Your first goal, if you're struggling for consistency and to make money, is to simply breakeven. The progression usually goes as follows: losing lots of money--> losing a little--> breakeven--> making a little money-->making lots of money. You cannot aspire to jump to the highest level directly if you're stuck in the lowest level. There is no jumping steps with trading. You need to put in the work and only focus on what you need to do next.

The calculation for this breakeven rate is fairly simple. If you're making 2R per win (that is, you're making on average, twice the amount you lose on average, everytime you have a winning trade), you will need a win percentage of around 35%. The calculation is pretty simple: say on 10 trades you win 3 and lose 7 with 2R per win. So your losses come to (7*1)= 7R. Your winners come to (3*2)= 6R. Your profit and loss is 6R-7R= -1R. So if you're risking 2% per trade, over 10 trades you can expect to lose 2% with this strategy.

Now, its important to note, when starting out, you will not have much of a base to calculate these numbers. You will need a minimum of 100 trades to reasonably calculate these ratios with accuracy. Therefore, my advice when you've placed under 100 trades is to risk as little as possible on your trades. I personally risk 0.5% per trade. There are a lot of trading authorities out there which say risking 2% per trade is perfectly fine but this is hogwash. You will find the vast majority of professional and successful traders risk anywhere from 0.25% to 1% per trade. The successful trader who risks 2% is an outlier.

Your first action upon reading that would probably have been to do some quick mental math and realize you cannot make millions a year with your capital size by doing that. This is indicative of a flawed mindset which needs some fixing. The good news is it doesn't take much to fix this. I'll address this in the next chapter on mindset and how to correctly think about success in trading. The truth is, the correct approach to trading is to constantly cover your downside all the time. Most people only think of the upside and their winners. The successful trader always covers risk and the downside before turning her attention to the upside.

Those of you familiar with the writings of Benjamin Graham may recognize this thought process. This is nothing but the "Margin of Safety" in action. This is a principle which is good enough for some of the greatest investors of all time. It ought to be good enough for you as well. There's no need to waste time reinventing the wheel. Just follow the process and you will get there. Those of you worrying about how you will get rich with this sort of trading, please be patient. I address this point in the final chapter.

Getting back to our quantitative look at risk, once you've placed atleast 100 trades risking under 0.25% per trade, you will be able to have relevant stats on your strategy and trade process. As I said previously, the win rate and R is the bare minimum you have to look at. You need to further dig into your numbers and understand the variance of your results. I'm not going to bore you with the statistical definition of variance but will instead illustrate what this practically means.

Let's say you're on a losing streak. Indeed if your trading strategy has a win rate of 35%, you will lose far more than you win and losing streaks of 2-3 trades are extremely likely. This is where struggling traders fail. Once the losing streak starts, they start tinkering with the strategy, assuming something is wrong. This is indicative of a Holy Grail mindset and as I've mentioned previously, this is completely the wrong way to go about trading. The correct approach is to understand what are the odds of such a losing steak occurring?

That is, with a 35% win rate, what are the odds of having a losing streak of 2 trades? 3 trades? 10 trades? I'm not going to disclose the answers to those questions here because once you search for them yourself, you're likely to be shocked. Briefly, it is extremely likely you will have a losing streak of atleast 8 trades with a win rate of 35%. Only when your losing streak becomes of such a size that it is improbable, should you start looking at your trade process. Until then, you need to remain aware of what your odds are at all times.

This is what it means to think in probabilities in trading. Most authorities simply make that statement and leave it hanging without further explanation. Trading is about being aware of your probabilities at all times. You may have noted in the section on the trading strategies, I never once indicated that any strategy is a sure shot or is foolproof. I even gave examples of when a given strategy fails. This is because I'm not concerned with how much of a sure shot a strategy is. I'm only concerned with what the win rate needs to be and how much R do I need to make on that strategy to make money. If I cannot make those numbers work for me after a sizeable sample, I drop it. This is how a professional thinks and it is crucial for you to adopt this method of thinking.

Understanding variance is a key part of evaluating your current strategy. Its not all doom and gloom though. For all the odds of a losing streak there are odds of a win streak as well. The number of wins in the streak will be smaller of course but when you factor in the 2R reward per win, you're making pretty good money on those streaks. I'll bet none of you will mind experiencing variance via a win streak. You shouldn't mind experiencing it via a losing streak either. This is an unnatural way of thinking and is something I'll address in the chapter on mindset.

Another key variable to look for is the consistency of your risk management. Now this can't be boiled down to a number but basically, you need to look at your losses and check if they are consistently around your risk percent per trade. So if you've decided to risk 0.25% of your account per trade, how many losing trades are actually at or below this number? If your losers are all over the place but average out to 0.25%, that is frankly, terrible risk management. It means you're likely adding to your losers and engaging in wishful and emotional thinking every time you enter a trade. The successful trader is someone whose losses show a consistent risk percentage of their account. So if they decide to risk 0.25%, their losses will be 0.25% or less. Enforcing discipline in this regard will do wonders for your strategy.

Another bogus piece of advice I've seen floating around recently is the thought that you should risk a fixed amount per trade versus a fixed percentage of your account. Risking a fixed amount violates the very basis of risk management which is covering your downside. It means in a losing streak you're actually risking a bigger percentage of your account and in a win streak you will be risking a smaller percentage as the streak lengthens. This is getting the worst of both worlds: losing more in a losing streak and winning less in a win streak. I really hope I don't need to further explain how stupid this piece of advice is. Some proponents of this method will argue it gets you out of drawdowns (that is, when your account balance dips below its peak equity value) faster. My response is, drawdown recovery is a function of variance, not some BS risk per trade formula.

Since we're on the subject, drawdowns are an important statistic to measure as well. No account in the world is on a continuous upward 45 degree angle. You will have peaks and valleys. A drawdown is essentially the length of that dip, measured as a percentage from the peak equity value and also as time, that is, measuring it in days and months. You will also need to measure recovery time which is the length of the upward swing past the old equity high from the bottom measured in days. A good system will have a faster recovery time as compared to the drawdown time.

The percentage of drawdown matters as well. As an FX trader, you should be aiming for less than 5% drawdown per month. If you're starting out, I recommend a drawdown limit of 3%. Yes, that is a limit. It means you will stop trading when you breach it. You need to have a drawdown limit for a day, week and month. Your daily limit can be defined as either a percentage or as the number of consecutive losses. For example if you lose 6 in a row, you cease trading for the day. I'm not saying 6 is a magic number, you will need to work out how much that means as a loss percentage given your risk per trade. Enforcing this requires discipline and awareness.

Violate this and you will not succeed. Its really as simple as that. If you're still not convinced consider this: Even Usain Bolt had bad days at the track. What makes you think you will have only good days in the market? Recognize when things are bad and exercise the option Bolt never had. You have the choice to take part or sit out.

Another informative statistic is the length of winners and losers measured as the time the trade was active. If your losers are far shorter in time than your winners, for example, perhaps you're placing your stops too close and not giving your trades room to breathe. Also look at how long your losers were in positive territory. If the majority of your losers, for example, tend to reach around 1.5R and then turn back, either your stops are too wide or perhaps you'd be better off targeting 1.5R instead of a higher ratio. You will be compensated because you'll have a higher win rate.

Qualitative Risk

Looking at risk qualitatively is a bit more difficult for beginners since most of them have never thought of risk in such terms or ever thought of risk as a function of discipline. Indeed most unsuccessful traders, whether beginners or experienced, tend to think of trading as having a successful strategy. They do not pay heed to risk management or mindset. They define an "edge" as how often the strategy wins or how much better it is or how it is some secret sauce that no one has discovered. The reality is, in this age of constant information, it is impossible for some secret sauce to exist indefinitely. Successful trading is indeed having an edge. Your edge, though, is made up of a number of things. It means executing your strategy perfectly. It means risking the correct amounts per trade. It means thinking the correct way about success (addressed in the next chapter).

Successfully executing this edge is a matter of preparation. Ask yourself, how well do you prepare for your trading day? Do you roll out of bed an hour before the open and sit down munching your breakfast and coffee while looking at your charts? Do you even consider things such as: How well did you sleep? How physically fit are you? What is your current mental state? Are you going through a tough period in your life that needs addressing? Have you practiced your technical skills?

Are you aware of how your weaknesses will attack you today? And so on.

Make no mistake, to trade successfully you need to approach your trading day with as much precision as an athlete approaches game day. Using the previous example of Usain Bolt, do you really think he ever showed up to a race hungover? Do you really think he didn't practice extensively before hand and execute his workout strategy? Do you think he ignored his nutrition needs? (notwithstanding his claim of eating Mcdonalds). Do you think he was out until 3 A.M the day before a race? Most of all, do you think he changed his methods of preparation simply because he was having a bad day? Do you think he did things differently before every race or did he do the exact same things over and over again?

These questions answer themselves. If you think you do not need to prepare for your trading day, you might as well flush your money down the toilet, you'll at least learn a lesson that way. Preparing well gives us confidence in our abilities and lessens the impact of losses since we know deep down there isn't anything we could have done better. It gives us a marker as to where our abilities are and what we need to do next. So what constitutes as good preparation?

To sum it up in a sentence: You need to ensure your mind is as close to its peak cognitive ability as possible. There will always be distractions and tough periods in our lives but you have to make sure you have a way to put them aside when trading. You need to evaluate if you have the ability to do this. The death of a loved one, for example, is impossible to put aside for most people. An argument with your spouse/girl/boyfriend though is somewhat more manageable for most. The point is you need to be aware of yourself and make a call. I highly recommend engaging in physical exercise and some form of meditation or mindfulness prior to the trading session. This ensures our bodies and minds get a workout and it refreshes us. I don't believe I need to go into detail about the benefits of exercise and meditation.

Ensure you get quality sleep every night. Do what you need to do to ensure this. If you miss exercising for a day, you can get by. Miss a night's sleep though and you're effectively a zombie. Take some time during the day to also practice your strategy.

There will be core elements to it and keep reinforcing and practicing these basics. Should you choose to follow the trend strength approach, you will need to constantly practice this skill in the beginning. The best way to practice is on a simulation software or on a demo account, although the latter is a bit slower in terms of reps received.

As you can see, not executing these steps correctly will leave you below your peak ability and trading without taking care of these things is akin to jumping into a sea of sharks with bloody meat strapped to you. Execute these to the best of your abilities and don't worry about anything else. If your mind is too unfocused simply walk away and come back the next day. The market won't go anywhere. If you choose to ignore this aspect, you're running huge risks and no amount of quantitative statistics will save you. There is a lot more to risk management than what I've outlined above and I will address this in a book later in this series. For now, consider the above a starting point and implement them immediately.

Executing all of this starts with your mindset which is what we'll look at next.

Chapter 10:
Mindset and Success

There is a belief prevalent in society that success in any field is a result of a person having some form of innate talent that they were born with. This belief causes us to think that if we don't have some magically presented talent towards something we are doomed to failure. A great writer is great because she was born having a talent for words, a musician was born with a talent for music and so on. This belief has completely warped our definition and expectations of success and has caused more failure than anything else.

Another toxic belief is one regarding hard work. Success, the belief goes, is a direct result of lots and lots of hard work. Put in the hard yards and its impossible to fail. There is some truth to this but in my experience, this statement overlooks a number of things, most specially, the nature of the work. People have been conditioned to believe now, because of these omissions, that mere hard work will guarantee success. In this age where computers are poised to take over a majority of low level jobs, nothing is further from the truth. Hard work is necessary, but it needs a proper channel.

Confidence is something else that is misunderstood. With regards to trading, confidence is something most struggling traders believe they will acquire once they start making money. They claim to not be confident in their strategy unless it makes them money. They build castles in the sky of how once they start making money, they'll execute flawlessly and manage risk well and live happily ever after. In the here and now though, they continue to lose money and keep blaming wrong strategies and the market and everything else under the sun.

These 3 qualities and beliefs, those regarding talent, hard work and confidence, underline our most basic beliefs about the world and ourselves. These beliefs exist on a sub conscious level and make themselves heard in ways which we cannot fathom unless we achieve a greater sense of awareness with regards to what is going on inside our minds. If you have the wrong beliefs, it doesn't matter what your strategy is or how good your risk management is, you will never be successful. Let's look at them one by one.

Talent and the need for it

How many times have you looked at a sportsperson doing something great and though "wow, they're incredibly talented" instead of thinking "wow, their mindset is so strong"? The harsh truth is talent doesn't count for much in the overall scheme of things. Sure, at the highest level of any endeavor, talent and genetics does provide a slight edge over the competition if everybody is executing at the same degree of efficiency. It does not however guarantee a path to success. The most talented person still needs to work hard. For example, most people look at the fact that Mozart became famous for his music at the age of 18 and put it down to some innate genius alone. The truth is, by the age of 18, Mozart had been composing music for over 13 years starting from the age of 5. He worked relentlessly on his craft and by the time he was 18, he was as experienced as any adult composer was. Thinking that Mozart simply rolled out of bed and became famous is absurd.

We recognize this absurdity on a conscious level but most of believe the exact opposite in our sub conscious minds. Guess what? It is our sub conscious minds that make up the majority of our thoughts, over 90% in fact. All of our actions are informed by the sub conscious and as long as you have this belief within you, you will continue to behave in ways that make it true. You will create a reality which conforms to your beliefs about the world.

The truth is, we do not need some God given gift to be successful traders. You do not need a math, science or financial background. Certain trading strategies do require you to be good at math and have an analytical background but the beauty of the markets are their diversity. You are free to adopt any strategy you choose. The success of that strategy depends on how perfectly you execute it, how well you manage risk and what you believe about yourself to be true. Where does talent come into that equation?

The world of sports is full of examples of conscious hard work triumphing over talent. If you're a fan of the NFL, you certainly know the story of Tom Brady. Here's a guy who went from being a scrawny backup on a team that had no wins in high school, to being the greatest QB of all time, supermodel wife and all. What do you think carried him to the highest level of his sport? Was it talent? Or was it his relentless pursuit of his vision and his willingness to execute whatever task was necessary? In the previous chapter, I outlined the basic outline of how to prepare for a trading day and the variety of ways in which you need to manage risk. If Brady were an unsuccessful trader, how do you think he would have reacted to that advice? How did you react to it when you first read it?

Michael Jordan, who needs no introduction, has repeatedly stressed how it was hard work and practice that made him the greatest. Not his talent. Trading is no different. You need to scrub this belief from you that you need to be talented to be a successful trader. We'll discuss some ways to install new beliefs at the end of this chapter but for now, please keep in mind that talent is overrated. It is perfect execution that always wins.

Hard Work and Success

Now there is no doubt that hard work brings success. Most people though develop an expectation of success just because they put in hard work. They end up working longer and more often and when success doesn't come they find themselves burned out and at their wits end. The reality is, hard work is but a part of the success formula. More pertinently, hard work done with the correct intention and towards the correct direction is what brings success.

You can sit there and stare at charts all day and consider it hard work. It certainly is. However, if you haven't decided on what it is you wish to achieve from looking at the charts, your work is of no use. You need to have a plan in place before you sit to work. Before you practice, you have to make a list of what your weaknesses are and work on those exclusively for that session. When you're trading the markets on demo prior to going live, you need to be conscious of what you're doing this for. You cannot tell yourself that you'll be more serious or execute better when you go live. Your execution has to be perfect and you need to do it repeatedly.

Hard work channeled in the right direction will always bring results. Now, there's no guarantee those results will be positive. However with a mindset that values learning over results, you will always move forward because you'll recognize even negative results make you stronger and better. Your work should be focused on improving your ability to execute better. So this means you train yourself to become an expert on your entry and exit signals, you train yourself to become aware of your thoughts and beliefs, you train yourself to implement methods to overcome or mitigate the harmful effects of said beliefs and you train yourself to be disciplined with your risk management. Directed this way, the work you put in will ensure your success.

Confidence

Much like unsuccessful traders think they'll magically execute better in realtime versus demo, many think they'll become confident in themselves and their strategy once the results start coming in. The reality is the other way round. Results come from the confidence in your abilities and your strategy. Using the previous example, do you think Tom Brady's confidence in himself dips when he throws an interception or loses a game? Do you think he starts thinking and adjusting his throwing mechanics when he tosses a pick? How about when he throws a touchdown? Does his confidence in himself rise or fall or does it remain the same as it was?

There's a valuable lesson here. Your results cannot dictate your confidence level in anything. Confidence need to be innate otherwise you'll be a slave to world and no one wants to be in that position, constantly rising and falling based on what others think of you. You need to have the belief that you will overcome challenges no matter the obstacle. Your mindset needs to be solution oriented, that is, you need to focus on the solution to your problems instead of the problems themselves and how they make you feel.

When under pressure, we tend to default to our ingrained mental programming. This means when you're trading, which is a pressure packed environment, you will default to your innate confidence level. If this is high, well and good, but if you're like most people, you'll start looking for results to justify feeling good about yourself and this leads to over trading, chasing wins and generally screwing up your strategy.

Focus on executing your strategy perfectly instead and focus on your belief in being able to overcome challenges, and you will achieve success. Below are some techniques to instill confidence in yourself and to root out toxic beliefs:

1) Visualize yourself being confident in the markets and executing flawlessly. Focus on things you can control.

2) Visualize accepting losses as cost of doing business and how your confidence level remains the same regardless of results.

3) If you aren't a visual person write out statements that confirm the above beliefs.

4) Prepare a trading plan which includes your plan to practice your skills and follow it.

5) Practice some form of meditation.

6) Start observing how you react under pressure. Observe and note down the symptoms. When they occur once more consciously turn your focus onto executing your strategy.

7) Inform someone close to you about your intent to eradicate incorrect beliefs. Have them prompt you anytime you say or do something which goes against what you want to achieve.

8) Practice gratitude.

The topic of mindset is a vast one and this along with risk management techniques will be addressed in greater detail in a future book in this series. The material outlined above, however, is a starting point and can be seen as the bedrock from which to build. You will always face challenges but remember, our response to the challenge is always a choice. Focus on what you can control and hope for the best with regards to what you cannot.

Chapter 11: How to Make Millions

Hopefully you've come to recognize how successful trading is a process and not some unattainable myth. Remember, you're always a lot closer than you believe. The key to successful trading is executing a number of steps flawlessly. If "flawlessly" seems a bit daunting, then remember that you can train yourself to do so. You don't need some special talent or secret ingredient to become successful.

Trading will offer you huge monetary rewards but most people have the wrong ideas as to the nature of those rewards. Let's get this out of the way first. You will not make a million within a year starting with a low 5 figure account. Consider this: the greatest investor of all time, Warren Buffett, has averaged a 20% annual return in his career. Let that sink in for a second. When anyone tells you they can sell you a system that guarantees 20% a month, run for the hills.

Don't be discouraged though. While you cannot live on 20% of a 10k account, if you establish a good track record which demonstrates excellent risk management and consistent execution, you will not have to go searching for capital. It will flow to you. Financial institutions are always on the lookout for good traders. By establishing a good track record (about a year) with your own money, you will demonstrate your ability to trade well and can apply for trading jobs at institutions and proprietary trading firms. The path to a professional trading career isn't that improbable coming from a retail trading background. Managing an 8 figure account within 3 years of a successful track record isn't far fetched. Do you think you can live on 20% of the gains of an 8 figure account?

All you need to do is follow the principles of successful trading as outlined previously. Focus on your execution and be aware of your mindset.

Last of all, have faith that the universe is looking out for you. You'll be fine no matter what happens. So remind yourself of that fact and get to work. I wish you the best of luck!

If you think this book has helped you gain any insight at all, please do leave a review on Amazon. I will sincerely appreciate your feedback.

www.ingramcontent.com/pod-product-compliance
Lightning Source LLC
Chambersburg PA
CBHW070152230526
45471CB00002B/634